I0438497

ONLY ONE GROUP CAN
SAVE AMERICA!

A 3 STEP PLAN TO CONVINCE CONGRESS
TO BEGIN MAKING DECISIONS
IN THE BEST INTEREST OF THE
AMERICAN VOTERS

Freddy Bishop

authorHOUSE®

AuthorHouse™
1663 Liberty Drive
Bloomington, IN 47403
www.authorhouse.com
Phone: 1-800-839-8640

First published by AuthorHouse   12/27/2011

ISBN: 978-1-4685-3209-8 (sc)
ISBN: 978-1-4685-3285-2 (ebk)

Library of Congress Control Number: 2011963086

Printed in the United States of America

Any people depicted in stock imagery provided by Thinkstock are models, and such images are being used for illustrative purposes only. Certain stock imagery © Thinkstock.

This book is printed on acid-free paper.

Because of the dynamic nature of the Internet, any web addresses or links contained in this book may have changed since publication and may no longer be valid. The views expressed in this work are solely those of the author and do not necessarily reflect the views of the publisher, and the publisher hereby disclaims any responsibility for them.

CONTENTS

I would like to dedicate this book to my wife, Cheryl, My daughter Jodi and her husband Curt, my son Nicholas whose interest in American politics and youthful courage inspired me to even try to put my thoughts into words, to the memory of my late father Wilfred Bishop Sr. and his two brothers Bernard and Conard, all three of which served the American Military on overseas battle fields during World War II with Conard also serving in the United States Army in Korea on the battle field during the Korean Conflict.

Step 1: Make Federal Election Day a National Holiday

Step 2: Use email, face book, and twitter to stay in touch with your Senator and Representatives in Congress

Step 3: Bring a new sheriff to Washington DC to clean up Corruption In the American Government

CHAPTER 1

America Is In Serious Trouble!

The Wall Street financial markets are no longer the stable forms of financial investments Americans used to depend on for their future or the future of our children and grandchildren. The jobs we enjoyed in the 50 years prior to 2010 have either been taken over by large business such as Wal-Mart, Walgreens and Krogers or moved overseas to reduce the production cost. The average American can no longer dream of making a living for their family by owning their own business as we did in the 1950's and 1960's particularly in rural areas of America. The Mom & Pop type grocery store, the local gas station owner, the local drug store, the local hardware and local dry goods stores have almost disappeared. Many of the gas stations and mini mart type stores have been bought up by foreign owners from India.

The factory jobs of the 1950's through the early years of 2000 have almost all been sent to countries over seas where the labor is less expensive as these other countries do not have government programs such as Welfare, food stamps, or unemployment to care for it's people that can not find work. Many Americans can draw as much money from the U.S. government subsidies by staying home and doing nothing as the foreign employees make by working to manufacture products that are resold in the United States sending US dollars into foreign hands. Many of these former American manufacturing companies that have relocated, no longer pay income taxes in America as they once did. This continues to place financial tax burdens on the working Americans that are left.

Most politicians in Washington D.C. seem to agree that we need more jobs in America, but they can't seem to agree on any plan to create jobs.

CHAPTER 2

Health Care In America

The American health care system has made great progress in discovering new medical treatments for improving the health of Americans, but the health industry has changed over the past 50 years. In the past hospitals were generally non-profit organizations being operated by owners such as U.S. cities and counties as well as various church groups such as the Catholic's, Baptist, Methodist, and Presbyterian for the purpose of helping the people suffering from illness in this nation as a public service to the people. Over the past 60 years health care has turned into a highly profitable private business industry. The American Health Care system is currently making billions of dollars for its owners by treating the ill. To make matter's even worse, the health care industry owners use some of their profits from treating American's illness and suffering to lobby our Representatives and Senators in Washington D.C. for the purpose of creating additional legislation that will continue to provide the owners of the various business in the health care industry more and better ways to make money from the illness and suffering of the American people.

This also drives up the cost of health care insurance for the average American, making it difficult for many Americans to even be able to afford health care insurance. We work all our lives to accumulate our homes, then as we become older and begin experiencing problems with illness, we find we can't afford the health care we need. This problem causes many Americans to loose their family homes as these properties are sold by our children or the courts for the purpose of using the money we earned and saved over our lifetime to pay the health care expenses we incurred before our deaths.

Some of the banking organizations have even came out with a new type of home loan for Americans over the age of 62 that is called a reverse mortgage. The loan companies loan the Senior Citizens of American money on their home while the senior citizens are still living. The Senior Citizens can use this money to pay medical bills while still living but once their lives are over, someone other than their descendents end up owning the Senior Citizens property.

The health care industry has made a complete turn around from its original goals in the early years of America as non profit organizations for the purpose of helping people deal with their illness as they pass through this life on earth. The changes in the American health care industry over the past 50 to 60 years is a good example of what happens when some things are turned over to private business to operate. It is true that many things the government gets involved with would be better off in the hands of private industry or private business, but that statement does not apply to everything that goes on in America. These days the Health Care

Industry is "All About the Money". Not one politician in Washington D.C really has any plan to solve the health care problems in America because the politicians are making too much money from the health care lobbyist, therefore America's health care problems are only going to continue to get worse in the future!

The Health Care insurance cost is high because the cost of health care is high which is only common sense. However, our Washington politicians are discussing and fussing about laws on Health Care Insurance and never even mention the actual cost of Health Care in America. I sometimes wonder if that whole health care insurance debate was nothing more than a smoke screen for the American Public made up by members of Congress from both parties, in the Happy Hour room for the purpose of getting the heat off of the politicians over health care cost from the American Voters because Congress gets more lobbyist money from the health Care industry than they do from the Health Care Insurance industry.

The cost of health care and the ability for all Americans to obtain proper health care is a major problem in the United States, but our Washington D.C. leaders do not have any real plans to correct or improve proper health care for all Americans.

CHAPTER 3

Democrats And Republicans

As we approach another Presidential election in America, the Republicans claim the answer for America is to continue to give the wealthy the tax breaks they have been receiving for the past several years so the wealthy will use this money to create jobs in the United States. The Democrats claim the answer is to tax the wealthy and use that money to create jobs building roads and schools.

Neither the Republicans nor the Democrats say anything about the fact that neither of these ideas have worked very well during the past 10 years. The wealthy take their income tax savings and invest it overseas where it is more profitable for them due to the lower wages of foreign employees as well as lower operating cost. The jobs building roads and schools are temporary jobs that do not last for very long like the factory jobs did that Americans had in the 1950's through the 1990's. In the mid 90's both Democrats and Republicans passed the Nafta agreement sending millions of American jobs out of the United States to foreign lands overseas. Why?

I remember hearing the politicians talk on television while the Nafta agreement was being discussed. They said the American job market is changing from factory type work to service industry type positions using computers and technology to create jobs. The politicians forgot the basic principle that it takes all kinds of investments in a Wall Street person's portfolio to make the Wall Street trader successful just as it takes all different types of jobs in America to keep all Americans working.

It seems like our Washington D.C. politicians are making decisions based on how much money they will get personally, then try to figure out a way to explain it to American's when they should be making decisions based on what is the best option for the majority of Americans.

Recently, one Congressman even made the statement in a public speech in 2011 stating there is not a problem with the employment numbers in private sector jobs in America. He claims the problem is a shortage of public government jobs in America.

It seems like the nations leaders are completely out of touch with the real American people. The Washington D.C. politicians seem to talk and talk but in the end all they want to do is too play politics and improve their own personal positions. The democrats are afraid the republicans are going to get their way and the republicans are afraid the democrats are going to get the democrat's way so nothing that really benefits the Average American seems to ever get done. It is all just a game to the politicians while many Americans are struggling in poverty to survive each day.

CHAPTER 4

The American Dream, Is It Over?

As a result of the "great shushing sound" as Ross Pero called it, the United States now has the greatest percentage of citizens in the poverty class that America has experienced since the great depression. American un-employment is at almost 10 Percent. Our politicians are still saying the same old things without giving Americans any real answers to the problems American faces today.

Why, because the truth is the politicians in Washington are trying to forget that the U.S. Constitution and the American government were built around the principal of "By the People, Of the People and For the People". The American leaders of the past have been more concerned with the needs of big business, Wall Street, and foreign governments. Why, because these organizations have lobbyist contributing large amounts of money to the American Leaders' campaign funds, personal interest groups or paying the leaders large sums of money as "consulting fees. The American Congressmen and women have kept these cash flow incomes to them as quite and as low key as possible. Our politicians tell the American Voters one thing in their campaign promises while the politician's actions reflect a politician principal of "By the Politician, For the Politician and of the Politician."

Once these so-called leaders arrive in Washington there is very little effort to make the information of what is really going on behind the scenes available to the American Voter's knowledge. They even took America's young men and women to war based on incorrect information concerning weapons of mass destruction. The world is a better place without Sadam Hussein, but was it worth the cost of American lives and dollars all of which were spent based on incorrect intelligence information. The politicians do not seem to worry about their companies, corporations, and associates making billions of dollars from providing soldiers clothes, equipment, weapons, food and other necessities, as young Americans gave their lives fighting for what they believed was the safety of the families and their homes in the USA. The lives of American Solders, their families, and the American Tax Payers deserve better.

Today the political leaders of America have gotten America into a terrible tangled web of confusion which acts as a smoke screen or cover allowing the Washington politicians to play their political pork barrel type games from which the politicians, the lobbyist and the companies as well as individuals including some of the foreign country leaders receive great financial gains at the expense of the American Tax Payer while the majority of Americans continue to suffer and struggle to survive from day to day.

It is really just the same old story we have heard before of how the Kings and Queens of Europe lived in wealth while the Average people of the country worked and struggled to survive in poverty while paying taxes to the rulers for their financial wealth and well being. The Kings and Queens did not want to let their subjects within the kingdom improve living and financial conditions too much as it would make the subjects more difficult for the Kings and Queens to control.

Growing up in the 1960's and 1970's the general dream of all Americans was the hope that our lives would improve in the future and the future of America would continue to improve for our children and grandchildren. Americans wanted to feel like the results of their hard work and planning as parents would be worth it as we watched our children and grandchildren grow and develop. Now in 2011, I hear the statement being made over and over that people are fearful of having children because America is in such a State of turmoil and confusion. The American parent's hope of a better future for their children and grandchildren has turned into fear and depression over what problems the future holds.

The two main political parties that control America have lost touch with the "Grass Roots American" that once made America Strong. The Republican Party has the basic idea that if the wealthy have money, they will hire employees build businesses creating work and the money will trickle down, keeping the American economy healthy and strong. The Democrats believe that the money should be given to the poor and they will spend it, putting the money back into the American economy creating jobs in America and therefore keeping American economically strong.

Well it seems like both parties can not seem to see the forest for the trees". The wealthy seems to be investing their money in overseas companies and Swiss bank accounts failing to let it trickle down to the average Americans. When the average American receives money, they have to purchase the items that will make their money go as far as possible, so they wind up buying products manufactured on foreign soil by foreign owned business creating jobs and wealth in the foreign countries economy rather than here at home in the United States.

Both Democrats and Republicans seem to have lost touch with the impact that foreign trade and balance of imports and exports seem to have on the American economy. It seems like the American leaders have bent over backward to let American jobs be moved overseas while taking billions of the working Americans tax dollars and giving it to foreign countries as Aide.

No economic plan will save America until the plan is based on the simple truth! There has to be more money coming into America than money going out of America. The American politicians of both parties need to focus all their attention on that principal idea and work to correct the damage that has already been done.

CHAPTER 5

American's Right To Vote For Its Leaders

Over the past 20 years many of the actions of America's political leaders has seemed like America's leaders have been more concerned with creating a one world government with their group being the leaders of the world rather than being concerned for the health and welfare of the American People.

When I attended elementary school in a small rural community, the general idea was that the first items of the day were to say the pledge of allegiance to the American Flag and pray the Lord's Prayer. The school teachers were just regular people none of which ever went to the high society colleges in America, but they all seemed to take pride in talking about being an

American Patriot, the difficulties they lived through during World War II as well as the difficulties of their parents and grandparents living through World War I. These teachers pointed out the main difference between America and other countries is, "American's right to vote" and elect it's leaders.

Many Americans that grew up in the first 50 years of the 20th century during World War I and World War II suffered hardships and loss of family and friends. Many of our Grandfathers, Fathers, Mothers and Children have given their lives in battle just to make sure Americans retained their "Right to Vote" During the last 50 years of the 20th century it seems like the "Right to Vote" is talked about less and less as has been the theme in America with some people trying to stop prayer in school, take the words "Under God" out of the Pledge to the American Flag, and even make it wrong for the 10 commandments to be displayed in public buildings. There has been a push to celebrate Christmas by saying "Happy Holidays'" rather than "Merry Christmas" Christmas cards,

School Plays, and other local public Christmas events in communities throughout America have experienced some pressure to remove the Christ out of Christmas and go for Happy Holidays. Wal-Mart and other department stores have even stopped selling the outdoor Nativity Scene displays! I think history has already proven that any nation that has forgotten God does not last!

I have heard a lot of discussion on television news programs about the difference between the various classes of people in the United States from the wealthy class, to the middle class, and those in poverty. The people living in the poverty class are jealous of those in the middle class, the people living in the middle class or jealous of the wealthy, and the wealthy are afraid that the poverty class and the middle class will get some of the wealth's money and improve their class in life. It still sounds similar to the problems of years ago with the Kings, Queens, and their subjects. However, there is one major difference in America that was given to us by our forefathers and ancestors that changes our circumstances from the days of

Kings and Queens if we as the American people will use it. That difference is our "Right to Vote" to elect the leaders of America. It does not matter if you are the poorest person in America, at the bottom level of the middle class income, at the top level of middle class income, or the wealthiest man or woman in America, your "Right to Vote" makes all Americans equal. There is one vote for one American and each vote is of the same value and counted the same. The wealthiest' person's vote is not worth any more than the poorest person's vote. The "Right to Vote" is what has made America the greatest nation on earth in the past, however many Americans have been failing to exercise their "Right to Vote" in the past. This is one of America's biggest problems!

As a child, I remember hearing my parents and their friends make the statement that "If an honest person gets elected to Congress they are turned into crooks when they get to Washington D.C. All our leaders in Washington D.C. are human beings and temptation is great. Once they see Lobbyist waving money in front of them, and they realize that that many

Americans are fussing about Washington D.C. but failing to vote and spend the time to check on what their leaders in the federal government are actually doing, the leader probably comes to the conclusion of "well why not".

There are 435 members in the United States House of Representatives and 100 members in the Senate for a total of only 535 national leaders in the American Congress plus our President and Vice President for a grand total of 537 men and women that are responsible for making the decisions needed to operate and conduct the business of the United States of America. There is no doubt that all the wealthiest corporations, business, and individuals in the world as well as foreign nations with dollars to spend are all after these 537 people trying to convince the American leaders to give these wealthiest corporations, companies, individuals, and foreign governments whatever it is that these groups are seeking that will benefit them the most.

On the other hand there is the American Voter that elects the leaders, but the truth is we are lucky if half of the eligible American Voters show up at the polls to vote, if the outside weather is good. If on Election Day the outside weather happened to be cold, snowy or raining, we might not even get more than half the eligible American voters to the polls. For the majority of the American Voters that do vote, once our vote is cast, we go on with our busy life's dealing with our own problems, verbally complaining about what we hear on the news in the afternoon when we arrive home, tired after a long day at work, but we never actually take any action to complain to our Representative or Senator in Congress about what we see going on in Washington D.C. This is the current situation in America, and it is a recipe for failure!

In the foreign countries of the Middle East, people are suffering and fighting to have the right to elect their leaders, rights that Americans already have. The creators of the American Constitution were extremely intelligent men creating the laws and rules for this nation, but I personally think that they suffered and fought so hard for freedom, as well as the right to vote, that it never dawned on them that all Americans would not exercise their right to vote in the future.

If America has any chance of surviving for our children and grandchildren, it is going to be because all Americans begin to exercise their "Right to Vote" and spend some time and effort in keeping up with what their Leaders in Washington D.C. are doing. **The American voters must turn the tables in Washington D.C. to let our leaders know that they are working for the American Voter, not the lobbyist, wealthy corporations, and foreign governments.** If the American Voter does not get this done, then we are letting 537 people give our nation away!

CHAPTER 6

Housing Market In America

With many Americans either facing or already experiencing foreclosure on their homes it does not look like the future is going to improve the housing market very much for the average American and especially young Americans with low paying jobs. Currently the Democrats are trying to use our tax dollars to subsidize some of the home owner's interest and payments so they can refinance at lower interest rates thereby obtaining lower monthly payments. The questions is how many people will this actually help and is this plan a long term solution or only a bandage attempt? One Republican presidential candidate said he would not do any thing about the housing market but just let the private investors purchase the housing at good prices, then rent them out to Americans. However the questions for his plan are: One: Americans have to have income in order to pay rent. Two: Why would any investor purchase a house for renting income if the income from renting was not greater than the cost of the purchase?

The story of how home loans have been handled and processed in America over the last 15 years sounds similar to the children's story where the Wicked Witch dropped candy and sweets in front of the small boy and girl to lure them into her home where she planned to cook them for dinner. The Banks made it easy for the Average Americans to borrow funds to purchase homes that were larger and more expensive than the previous generation. With home loans and down payment loans being dangled in front of Americans in need of homes like the candy and sweets in the children's story, many home buyers made larger purchases than they should have. With so many homes being purchased it drove the price of housing up. When the bankers game had finally ran it's course and home loans were not being paid back, one of those same bankers happen to have been appointed to a federal government political position where he encouraged our leaders to borrow money from China to bail out the banks from disaster, again placing the burden on American tax dollars for the banking industry's game. Once that occurred, the value of the American homes began falling drastically. Now that the home values are less than what the average American owes on the loan, the best idea is supposed to be let investors buy the property and rent it to the Average American.

How can the Average American possibly win and prosper in the future when these types of games are being played by the American politicians? I can't help but think that the home loan situation in America did not just happen by accident but was a planned event by the large banks and politicians in America to make money for themselves and continue to bleed the American tax payer's dollars!

Once again it seems like the political leaders can not see the forest for the trees. They need to be working on plans to increase jobs and incomes for the Average

Americans so Americans can make enough money to own their homes and have a prosperous live of their own in their own home, not existing as a renter paying money to some rich investors. The games being played today continue to remind me of the days of Kings and Poppers in Europe. Is America headed back in the direction of over 350 years ago into the same economic type of conditions that drove the Pilgrims to go through so many hardships to settle in the New World?

CHAPTER 7

Why Does America's Leaders Want To Cut Spending On The American People Rather Than Cut Tax Dollars Being Sent To Foreign Governments?

America's political leaders should have put together a super committee of Congress persons to determine how to increase jobs and income for all Americans instead of putting together a super committee of our leaders to determine how to cut spending in American. What is even worse is that most of the spending cuts will probably be on Medicare health cost for elderly Americans, spending on education for American Children, and cuts that will affect the Average American but not the Wealthy American.

Why are the political leaders not considering ways to increase revenue by raising import taxes on goods shipped in from other countries, making it easier for the American worker to compete in pricing of products? Why are the political leaders not trying to come up with ideas and solutions that will balance the average income of Americans to the actual cost of living in this country. Why are the political leaders not increasing minimum wage, and decreasing the unemployment benefit so the Average American will make more money working than they do staying at home drawing unemployment, and letting the illegal Mexicans do the work? The unemployment and alien labor problems have been handled so poorly by our political leaders that the farmers are now having problems finding an American work force to gather their crops because the government has been running the illegal aliens out of the country, while continuing to provide unemployment benefits to unemployed American workers who would wind up making almost as much if not more drawing unemployment than they would by working for the farmers. All of this going on and the American unemployment rate is still high. The American political leaders are just plain not doing a good job when it comes to finding common sense solutions for America's various problems.

Why are the politicians trying to cut Welfare, rather than change the Welfare rules that allow some Americans to take advantage of the system when it is only driving the tax dollars up for the Average Working American? Why are the politicians trying to put Social Security in the hands of private industry, when we have already seen that the private industry is only interested in making money for itself. Social Security is too important for Americans to let just a few wealthy Wall Street players bleed the Social Security monies off for themselves.

Why are our political leaders not investing tax dollars in government owned (American Voter Owned) factories to build Solar power Panels and accessories, natural gas equipment for CNG, and equipment to improve the production of electric cars to reduce America's dependence on foreign oil rather than making large loans to private industry for these purposes allowing the private industries to once again, bleed the Average American of their tax dollars by spending the loan then filling bankruptcy leaving the taxpayer holding the bag.

Less government is not always the answer, but sometimes you have to have rules and control over the process especially when money is involved. The reason politicians keep saying put the money in private industry is because that is a game were the politicians have a chance for them and their friends to get their hands on the American Tax dollars for their own benefit and personal gain. It has turned into a Washington Game to see who can get as many tax dollars as possible by inventing a method of distributing grants and government backed loans to private industry. The American Tax dollars should never be given to private industry to use either in the form of a loan or grant. Private industry should stand on its own dollars.

Why are the Political leaders of America all shouting cut spending to solve the American budget, but no one seems to be making any effort to figure out how to increase income in America. Any good business person knows that you have to work just as hard to increase income as you work to reduce spending in a successful business.

The political leaders of America are intelligent, highly educated men and women, why are they not working on grass root foundation solutions to the American economic problems rather than running around putting out some sort of smoke screen, trying to create as much confusion for the Average American as possible, allowing the politicians to play their Washington games hiding behind the smoke screen for cover. The Washington game is the political game about Money and who can obtain the most of it. It has lost the original intention of our forefathers "By the People, Of the People, and For the People".

CHAPTER 8

The American Tax Code

The average American cannot understand the American tax code which is approximately a 3000 page document of rules and regulations that have been altered and changed by America's political leaders over the history of America mostly to benefit the tax deduction needs of the Americans and companies doing business in America that have been large contributors to the various political campaigns. As a result of these political changes the Average American now pays a larger percentage of his income for taxes than the wealthy Americans. This continues to sound a lot like the stories I used to read and watch on TV as a child about the Kings or rulers of a country would place heavy tax burdens on the working class citizens while the Kings and their friends lived a much easier life style. We now live in a tremendously more modern world than in those old days, but it still seems like the more things change, the more they remain the same.

Maybe it is true that history repeats itself. The American tax code is in such a mess that only 51% of Americans even pay income tax. I would guess that the majority of the American tax dollars that the politicians are spending faster than it is coming in, are paid by the Average American. It does not take a rocket scientist to realize that the current tax code needs to be thrown out the window and completely changed into a tax code that would be fair for all Americans. In the real world, if any business employee proposed a business plan as confusing and unfair as the current American tax code, the owner of that business would dismiss the employee from the company, but in Washington D.C. our leaders believe it is all just good politics.

CHAPTER 9

The American Budget

Our previous leaders over the past several years, as well as our current leaders are having trouble coming to an agreement on how to budget the spending of the tax dollars paid by the American people. They discuss and discuss it but neither the Democrats nor Republican can seem to agree with each other. Surely they all understand that any financial institution whether it is a business or an American Family budget cannot survive for an extended period of time when they or spending more money than they are taking in. Yet our leaders have gotten America so far in Debt that a bankrupt America is not out of the question in the future. As a matter of opinion, I think if the American politicians do not balance the budget in a common sense manner rather than based on not hurting their political campaign contributors America is destine for Bankruptcy in the future.

This will not be a good situation for the majority of Americans because we will be struggling to survive even more so than we are now. Citizens of Foreign countries that are financially strong will be buying up American property as is already the case. With the value of our property dropping, the wealthy will be able to own more and control more. This also makes me continue to think about history in the days when the Kings ruled the country rather than the country being a democratic government. Anyone can easily figure out that Congress has failed and continues to fail to manage the American Tax payer's dollars in a reasonable, responsible and Professional manner.

CHAPTER 10

Welfare

The Welfare system has a honorable purpose, but the American politician has played with the rules so much that 45% of Americans are not paying any taxes but receive some type of government checks. Much honest work needs to be done by honest and sincere leaders to correct the many problems of the Welfare system,

CHAPTER 11

The American Debt

In the year ending in 2001 the total American debt was about $5.8 Trillion dollars. In the year ending 2011 the total American debt has increased to $15.2 Trillion dollars. During the George W. Bush administration, the American Debt tripled and it seems to be growing just as quickly under the Bracha Obama Administration. **During the first 225 years of American's History the leaders of our nation accumulated a total debt of approximately $5.8 trillion. During the last 10 years that total debt has increase to over $15.2 trillion**.

The current United States budget indicates the US is estimating a deficit of around $1.3 trillion in

2012 which will push our gross debt total to well over $16 Trillion next year.

For America's leaders to accumulate triple the amount of U.S. debt that our leaders acquired during the first 225 years of this nations history in just the last 10 years should be a Major Red Flag to the American Tax Payer that something is terribly wrong with the politicians in Washington D.C. History has proven that the Roman Empire fell because it was bankrupted by its leaders. It looks like the American leaders including the Congress and not just the President are blind to the fact that they are driving America toward Bankruptcy as the Roman leaders did.

America's first President, George Washington, made this statement concerning America's Debt in his Farewell Address to the nation on September 17, 1796 . . . . *Use public credit sparingly! Bear in mind that towards payments of debt there must be Revenue, that to have Revenue there must be taxes; that no taxes can be devised, which are not inconvenient and unpleasant!*

Every time America borrows $1.00 from China, which is $1.00 of our tax dollars that we are going to have to send China plus the interest on the loan. The U.S. currently owes China $1.5 Trillion dollars or about 10% of the total American Debt.

Yet while we continue to borrow money to operate America at a rate faster than we are gaining revenue, our political leaders talk about cutting Medicare health benefits for our Senior Americans, and reducing the Military budget. America's political leaders never seem to mention cutting the trillions of dollars that we are sending overseas to foreign governments for the so called purpose of buying friends. Our leaders continue to borrow money from China sending America closer to bankruptcy while our leaders are in essence spending those borrowed funds outside the U.S. borders when our tax dollar revenue is still less than the budget. Those foreign governments receiving American's Future tax dollars that we owe China, must have a lot better lobbyist in Washington working with the American politicians that America's Senior Citizens and America's Military does.

It would be interesting if someone actually knew how much of America's tax dollars is being sent to foreign Countries, the amount of those dollars that never make it past the foreign countries leaders, as well as how much the foreign lobbyist pay American's leaders to make decisions to send this money overseas.

America's first president, George Washington, warns America against permanent foreign Alliances which could lead to foreign influence and corruption in his farewell address on September 17, 1796.

As a child growing up in the late 1950's and early 1960's I remember my parents talking about how so many different products that they were purchasing in the United States were made in China. Apparently China's imports into American increased tremendously after World War II. After I look back to listening to those "Made in China" comments, it makes me wonder if once China's income from Americans began to accumulate, the leaders of China got the idea to encourage America's Politician's to send money over seas to other foreign governments, buy more and more products from China, with the long term goal of owning the American government someday. Is America's debt to China just something that accidently happened over the last 50 years due to poor management of America's assets by America's leaders or was this problem a planned problem as China realized how easily American's leaders can be influenced with lobbyist money.

If the individual American Voter does not stand up, exercise their right to vote each election, and begin paying attention to our political leader's actions, then the future of America is in tremendous jeopardy. Americans must make an effort to contact their state's Congressional Senators and Congressional Representatives, letting them know that the leaders must balance America's loans from China and all other sources to America's Revenue from America's tax dollars. It only makes common sense for our Political leaders to cut out spending money overseas before they begin cutting out spending here in America. American's are going to have to realize that if they want America to remain the United States of America, rather than the United States of China, Americans must make as many purchases from American made products as possible and reduce the purchase of products manufactured overseas. When Americans purchase goods made in other countries we are actually shooting ourselves in the foot if you think about it.

American's Workers Union's should be spending efforts to figure out how American's manufacture's can compete with foreign manufacturing concerning operating cost as well as product quality. American's should also consider telling our political leaders that increasing the important taxes on items made overseas should be considered as a way of increasing America's Revenue rather than increasing the tax dollars that American's are paying. The American Voter must become very knowledgeable on America's foreign trade problems so that they will not be swayed by political statements trying to create confusion for the American Voter so corruption can continue until America finally goes bankrupt. The American Voter must keep in contact with the Washington Politicians in order to protect America from financial corruption of our tax dollars.

There are several web sites that will provide the American Taxpayer information on government spending. One such site www.usgovernment spending.com has a great deal of information to help the average American tax payer learn more about how American tax dollars are being spent.

CHAPTER 12

Energy In America And The Epa

When you think about America's energy needs and drive down most Federal Interstates in America, it is pretty amazing to think that enough gasoline and energy for making electricity can even be produced by the entire world and delivered into America to keep Americans moving. Every where you look there are cars and trucks running up and down the road. American can not move around this nation as we do without the fuel from other countries. However, when you consider that Americans figured out how to place a man on the moon in a little more than 60 years after the Wright brothers' first flight, it is difficult to understand why our demand for energy has not been managed better.

America has pretty much been kept dependent on receiving energy from the Middle East, which has gotten us into the Gulf War, The Iraq War, The Afghanistan war, all of which has cost American lives and American tax dollars. When I was a child, I remember hearing my uncle talk about a vehicle carburetor that would achieve gasoline consumption of 60 mile for every one gallon of gasoline when installed in a large Cadillac car. The story goes that the person who invented this carburetor was approached by a large oil company and purchased the rights to manufacture this carburetor which was never heard from again. Having spent over 30 years working in the natural gas industry, I know that natural gas vehicles have been possible since the early 1980's and probably even before, yet here in America, the EPA has some strict testing requirements that are tremendously expensive, so this hampers the use of natural gas as a vehicle fuel in America. Well, to my knowledge, I believe natural gas burns cleaner than gasoline, so why is the EPA continuing to have regulations that are road blocks to using natural gas as a vehicle fuel making America less dependent on foreign oil? In Venezuela, over 90% of the vehicles run on natural gas. The reason is because there is more profit in selling the Venezuela oil to America than there is profit in turning the natural gas into LNG and shipping natural gas to America. Using their common sense, Venezuela runs most of their vehicles on natural gas sending their oil to America obtaining more American dollars that way.

There are also a great deal of EPA regulations on drilling for oil and gas in America. Some are necessary, but some or just plane overboard. In any case, the end result is that EPA and other government regulations make America more dependent on foreign oil.

The EPA has about destroyed the coal industry over the past 50 years. When I was a child, coal mining was a big business, but due to environmental regulations the use of coal has about been ran out of America. However, the Coal industry advertises on television that they have developed ways of burning coal in a cleaner operation than in the past so why is the use of coal not being supported more than it is.

Because the use of coal would make Americans less dependent on foreign oil.

Solar Power is also a realist way to generate energy for your home, however this equipment is not being massed produced in America so the cost of buying Solar Power equipment makes Solar Power about a 17 year return on the home owner's investment before breaking even. The U.S. government gets involved and guarantees a loan to a Solar Power equipment producer who runs through the money, then files bankruptcy, leaving the American tax payer hanging. Why does someone in government not come up with a way to encourage some private investor to begin mass producing Solar power equipment by working out a set price for the product then giving the American tax payer that purchases the equipment a tax break that make the use of Solar Power in homes an immediate first year savings verse the cost of electricity. America's leaders are surely smart enough to figure out how to accomplish increasing the use of Solar Power if they really wanted to.

Private industry wants to construct a pipeline from Canada to the United States to deliver Canadian Oil to us, but the United States President wants to put off any decisions until after next years election. Again, this is something that would not cost the American taxpayer, create American jobs, make America less dependent on foreign oil, but is being held up, keeping America as dependent on foreign oil as possible.

America needs so much energy, that we will never be totally energy independent, but solar power, natural gas vehicles, electric vehicles, and the use of coal to operate large electric generators could all work together to greatly decrease America's dependence on Foreign oil but there always seems to be a road block of some type coming from the American Government that stops these other forms of energy from being developed. Why, probably because the Foreign Oil producing countries have encouraged the American leaders to find ways to keep those road blocks coming so we will be as dependent on foreign oil as possible. It is difficult to keep from thinking that the United States' Environmental Protection Agency is being influenced by the oil producing nations in the Middle East such as Saudi Arabia.

When you think about the American lives that have been lost in battle, the America earned dollars that have gone to the foreign oil producers for American fuel, and the cost of the wars America has fought over foreign oil, America's leaders have been doing an extremely poor job managing America's energy needs the past 40 years. It looks like our leaders have tried to help keep America as dependent on foreign oil as they can when they should have been working to develop other sources of fuel such as solar power, natural gas and electric vehicles. It is also possible to blend propane with diesel to improve the performance of an engine. As a lot of propane is being produced in the United States from the abundant supply of natural gas that we have, this form of energy could also help the U.S. be less dependent on foreign oil, but I never hear anyone talking about it. I think Ronald

Regan was the greatest President that America has had in my lifetime, but even he ordered the solar power panels removed from the White House when he was President.

I am afraid America's leaders may have been as well as continue to be too friendly with the oil producing Saudi Arabia. Even Osama bin Laden was from one of the wealthiest Saudi Arabia families. His actions against the United States on September 11, 2001 is the reason America went to war in Afghanistan, costing the lives of American Soldiers and billions of American tax dollars to fund those wars. It is difficult for me not to wonder as well as worry if all that has happened to America since September 11, 2001, the wars, the Americans killed in battle, as well as the tremendous increase in the American debt has all happened by chance, or has it been the execution of a plan from the wealthy oil producers and leaders in Saudi Arabia. I pray that it has all happened by chance. I would hate to wake up some morning to find out that the wealthy oil families of Saudi Arabia have purchased up all of America's Debt and were planning to continue to fund our budget deficit adding to what we owe them so they could call us the United States of Saudi Arabia rather than America.

CHAPTER 13

The American Voters

American television has about 6 or 8 TV stations that broadcast current news and political information 24 hours per day. Some Americans watch these stations constantly while other Americans feel like everything in American politics and government is so messed up they don't want to even think about the days political events unless they have too, in order to avoid becoming depressed. Each news TV station is generally owned by either a Republican or a Democrat so the news casters generally try to sway their viewers in the direction of their political party. Newspapers have been the same political news organizations over the years as the current TV news stations.

Lots of people are talking on the news channels with several opinions on the various political situations, America's financial problems, America's problems in dealing with foreign countries and so forth, but the Average American has lost hope of being able to do anything about our nation's current circumstances. Only about 60% of us even vote in the federal government elections. The remaining 40% of American voters have either given up or have an illness that will not allow them to visit the voting polls on Election Day.

The Average American that does vote in federal elections usually goes home after voting and that is basically all they really do as far as having a part in how the American Government is operated. Once the various candidates are elected, they go to Washington D.C. and do what they want to. What they want to do seems to be making the people happy that gave the politician campaign money. The only real say the Average American has is their vote on Election Day and then the Average American is out of the game.

To the political leaders in Washington D.C. it is all about the money, when it should be all about the American people. As of November 04, 2011 it was stated on one news program that the members of the U.S. Congress personal wealth has increased by 25% of the past two years while the average personal wealth of the Average American has probably decreased. American is on a political spending roll-a-coaster that has gone completely out of control and in such a mess with so many different interest groups pulling in so many different directions, the problems can not be resolved by either political party, the President or anyone in the entire United States. The U.S. Economy is in such a shambles that the only group that can save America is the group that is paying most of the tax dollars "The Average or Regular American Voter"!

It is time for the Average American Voter to stand up, putting forth the time and effort into keeping informed on the events that are being discussed in Washington D.C. by American's leaders. The Average American can no longer afford to just vote on Election Day, then walk away and just verbally complain until time for the next election. Now is time for the Average American Voter to realize that just as our fathers, grandfathers, mothers, grandmothers, our children and other ancestors have fought wars on foreign soil, suffering all types of hardships with many of them giving their lives in battle, from the landing of the Pilgrims in America through the Revolutionary War, the Civil War, World Wars I and II, Viet man, Korean War, as well in the Middle East wars over the past 20 years, in order to give us the opportunity to live in a free nation, we the voters must stand up.

The Average American Voters are going to have to stand up and fight a political battle to change the way the American politicians conduct the business of America. The Average American Voter has paid more than their fair share of the American tax dollars, but The Average American Voter has not really had much of a voice in Washing D.C. Once the political leaders take office, they are pulled and enticed by the large money lobbyist from large corporations and foreign countries as well. The only time the political leaders pay much attention to what the Average American Voter needs is right before an election, but the politicians seem to forget who elected them somewhere along the way on their trip between the politician's home state and Washington D.C. The politician seems to say what we want to here before election, then try as hard as possible to "keep quite and keep a low profile" once they are in office so they can put as much money in their own pockets as possible without being noticed by the Average American Voters back home.

CHAPTER 14

America's New Communication Abilities Combined With The "Right To Vote"

During the first 200 years of America's history it has been easy for the American Politicians to get away with taking advantage of the Average American Voter as there were only three forms of communication, newspapers, letters, and verbal speeches until the early 1900's when radio began, then in the early 1950's televisions first begin to show up in the Average American's home. Newspapers, radio, and television improved the information the Average American received concerning world events and American Politics, but these forms of communication did not give the Average American any way to express their thoughts, opinions, and concerns back to the politicians in Washington D.C. All the Average American could do was to listen and absorb what is going on in Washington as well as around the world.

In listening over the last 60 to 70 years, the mess that has been created by the American politicians in Washington D.C. has basically killed the American Sprit of many Average Americans making them feel like American and the world is in such a state of confusion there is not a chance in the world the Average American can do anything to make a difference in American Politics.

But in today's world, with the invention of the internet, email, face book and twitter, a new form of communication is now showing up in many Average American's homes that give them the ability to instantly communicate to American's political leaders in Washington D.C. Now is the time, before it is too late, for the Average American to use these recently invented forms of communication to make the American Political leaders listen to the people of America rather than the rich lobbyist. The Founding Fathers of America gave the American people something in the Constitution of the United States that is more powerful than the lobbyist money and that gift is our "Right to Vote" for and select America's political leaders. The "Right to Vote", combined with the ability to instantly communicate to everyone across America with the internet, email, face book and twitter, are the tools that the Average American can use to change the current American political leaders into an honest government that is ***"By the People, Of the People and For the People"*** which is what the founding fathers of American intended when they started this Nation over 240 years ago.

The ability to instantly communicate the average Americans voice to the political Leaders in Washington D.C. is a tremendous tool that was not available during American's first 236 years. But it is here now and it is up to the Average American to use these communicating tools, spending time on learning what the issues are in Washington, discussing them with each other across the nation, and then communicate our personal and individual opinions to our own states representatives in Washington D.C. on a daily basis. Web sites such as Thomas(Library of Congress) Thomas.loc.gov, www.opengress.org, govtrack.us/congress/legislation, congresssummary. com, fib.com, www.politico.com, and opencongress. org are just a few of the web sites now available to keep the average American informed of the activities taking place in Washington D.C. Now Average Americans can make changes in Washington D.C. and the way the American political leaders conduct our nations business, spending our tax dollars if the Average American will take the time to stand up and make their thoughts and beliefs known. The Average American can use the power of instant communication across America along with the *"Power of the Vote"* to turn America around and head it in the right direction!

CHAPTER 15

A Three Step Plan For American Voters

With the American Voter consisting of so many different types of people who are spending their time dealing with the normal day to day struggles of life, just trying to raise their children, figure out how to deal with their money problems, deal with health issues of themselves or their family members, basically just trying to survive in today's world, it is easy for the politicians to manipulate our thoughts and attitudes concerning the issues about how the politicians spend our tax dollars.

"Divide and Conquer" has been a great plan of attach for war generals fighting physical battles since the beginning of time. This plan of attack also works

well in political battles. The American Voters must make every effort to come together as a nation to fight the day to day political battles just as our men and women in the military fight the physical battles in this world.

America is a great melting pot of many different people with different opinions, emotions, backgrounds, and goals. It is easy for the slick talking politician to keep the American people "Divided and Conquered" so that the politicians can spend America's tax dollars any way they want too in Washington D.C.

Americans are going to have to realize that voting as well as voicing our opinions to our leaders in Washington D.C is our duty as an American Citizens. We owe our efforts to keep up with current events and correspond with the Senator and Representatives from our individual states to past American Generations, to our own generation, and to future generations in America. We can not continue to let the politicians play the games in Washington D.C.

that could easily lead to destroying the United States of America's government, taking away our freedom in this generation as well as the freedom of future American generations. **Regardless of our various differences, Americans must realize that we are really all together in one boat called the United States of America and if that boat sinks, we all go down with it together!**

In order to get American Voters together, there are three basic steps that each American Voter should seriously consider taking in order to turn American politics around making our political leaders in Washington D.C. aware of the fact that the leaders job is to make decisions by listening to the American people's ideas rather than the ideas of the lobbyist flashing money around in the halls of the United States Congress!

Step #1 Make Federal Election Day a

National Holiday

Only about 38% of Americans voted in the 2010 federal elections and only 60 % voted in the 2008 federal election with the President position on the ballot. The 60% of voting Americans have to be acquainted in some form or manner with the remaining 40% of Americans that have not been voting in Federal Elections. Americans should encourage each other to vote by talking to family members, providing a car ride if needed so the voter can travel to the election polls on Election Day. Americans should check on the senior citizens in their neighborhoods that would not normally vote without having transportation to the election polls. The hospitals should think about their patient's rights to vote and provide some type of plan for early voting or absentee voting for hospital patients that would not normally have the opportunity to go the election polls on Election Day. Private Non Profit organizations such as Senior Citizens Clubs, Kwinana's, Lions Club, various hunting and gun clubs across America and many other organizations should be having goals of doing anything they can in their communities to encourage All Americans to vote.

Americans should be teaching their children about the importance of voting in all elections. The American Child needs to grow up realizing how special the "Right to Vote" in American is as well as the history of Americans that have fought, worked, and suffered to provide the American Citizens the "Right to Vote during the history of this nation. School systems should put a special emphasis on teaching children the importance of participating in each and every election. Employers should provide their employees a paid holiday on each Federal Election day. Election Day should be as important if not more important of a national holiday as the Fourth of July is.

All American voters need to realize that the problems with the politicians in Washington D.C. and the problems of this complex world we now live in have gotten to the point that if All Americans do not begin to exercise their "Right to Vote, Americans could very well loose that right for themselves and future generations.

In my lifetime I have observed that most elected officials really don't want to encourage voting as they believe the fewer votes cast, the better chance the official has of getting re-elected. Apparently "Keep a low profile" and "the less said the better" are common "*good old boy*" election winning strategies.

If you think about it, we very seldom, if ever hear an office holding federal official encouraging people to get out and vote on Election Day. Elected officials seem to think that being elected to a public office gives them the right to play games to serve the officials personal agenda rather than serve the people. These kind of political games have been going on since the first election was ever held in America, but as this nation has grown and developed over the years and the world has became smaller due to modern communication methods, so many games have been played by America's political leaders that it has placed our economy in great jeopardy. The future life style of our children and grandchildren is at great risk.

Before it is too late to make a change, every American needs to stand up and make a hard push to encourage all their family, friends, and acquaintances to vote on Election Day. Americans must do anything they can in their own particular situation to work for at least a 99% participation of American Voters exercising their power to vote. No government official is going to push this, companies and corporations are not going to say anything if they do not have too. Foreign countries are not going to encourage Americans to vote.

The only group that can save America is the American voter. Each American is going to have to do everything we can on our own, in our individual circumstances to make a never before seen effort to encourage voting in the Federal Elections anyway we can, at our homes, work locations, schools, and other organizations where we come in contact with other American Citizens.

Between 1775 and May 2011 408,306 Americans have been killed in battle with an additional 670,846 Americans wounded in battle to protect American citizens' freedom and the right to elect our leaders by the power of our vote. If the eligible voters in American do not exercise their voting privileges and use the new powers of communication that we currently have in the United States, we are surely letting those that were killed or wounded in battle to protect our freedom and voting privileges down. We cannot let this happen!

Each and every American should contact their Congressional Representative and Senator requesting a bill be passed in Congress that will make America's Federal Election day a national holiday, then Americans must get out and vote for the future of our children, grandchildren, and all future generations!

Step #2 American Voters use new

communication abilities.

As American Voters, we have to overcome the feeling that there is nothing we can do to change or help the political situations in Washington D. C. We must begin to keep in contact with the elected federal officials that represent our individual states in Washington D.C. American Voters must demand our elected officials to provide us with a web site, their email addresses, and some type of face book address or twitter address. We must demand that our elected officials maintain their own web site where our elected federal officials will keep us informed on a daily basis of the bills and discussions that the officials are currently involved with or working on.

Every American Voter the elected official represents from his or her home state should have the opportunity to check the politician's web site daily and make their own comments by email, face book, or twitter for the purpose of letting the elected official know how the American Voters in his or her state feel as American Voters on the current issue being discussed in Washington D.C. We need to realize that it is our responsibility as Americans to keep up with what is going on in Washington, discuss current issues using the new forms of communication we now have available to us. American Voters should make their comments known to our elected officials in Washington D.C on a daily basis. We can also use face book and twitter to discuss the various problems with our friends and neighbors as well as all across our own state. In addition to the state communications we should also have access through a face book or twitter system to discuss issues and find out what other Americans think about each situation. We all need to try to find common ground solutions for America's problems as well as try to understand what is best for all of America.

The American Voters should be demanding that our federal and state governments use the new communication forms to provide American Voters this type of system to discuss issues with each other and with our elected officials of each state. The elected officials should be making decisions on the American voter's opinions and ideas rather than the large companies and foreign government lobbyist desires. The so called lobbyist need to be trying to convince the American Voters of what is best all of America helping the American Voters to find common ground solutions while earning the voters support. The political lobbyist could buy advertising on the political face book type form of communication, as well as by using their dollars and large corporate support to create good jobs in America rather than using their money to pay off the congress or supporting the congressional campaigns in order to get the lobbyist desired goals.

The American Voters must contact their congress person often enough to change Washington D.C. and the way our nation's business is being conducted.

America can not survive in today's world if only 60% of the eligible voters participate in an election, then send the elected official to Washington D.C. where he or she is then controlled by the money from the various lobbyist in Washington D.C. Americans must keep track of how the Senators or Representatives from their individual states vote on each issue before Congress. The America Voters must turn the way Congress thinks around by letting the elected officials know that if their actions are not what is the best for the majority of American people, then they will not be getting our vote in the next election.

Various web sites exist that will give you information on how to contact your Congress person by email or mail. A few of those are www.contactingthecongress. org as well www.senateconservatives and www.house. gov/writerep.

You can check up on various political issues by pulling up the web sites of Fox, ABC, and CBS, NBC news programs as well as various web sites for individual programs such as "Varney and Company" Willis and Company and many others including a government web site "The Public Notice.org".

As American Voters we must begin to use the "Power of the Vote" so many of our ancestors have fought battles for, given their lives for, as well as faced much suffering for. We must change the way Congress makes decisions by making them listen to us, the American Voter, rather than by making their decisions based on which lobbyist gives the elected official the most money.

American Voters must take the time and effort to let our elected officials know that we elected them to represent us, the voters, when they go to Washington D.C. rather than to become personally wealthy by taking money from the lobbyist.

Step #3 Keep up with what Congress is actually doing and let them know we will be voting in the upcoming elections.

There are approximately 236,000,000 eligible voters in America. That immense voting power can make a difference if we can keep the politicians from making Americans think the politician is doing one thing when they talk about running for election but actually doing the complete opposite once the politician arrives in Washington D.C . . . The ethics of Congress is based on a policy written by Congress, controlled by the Congressional ethics committee made up of current congressional office holders, and usually works for the benefit of the politician as it normally happens in Washington D.C. The American Voter needs to use their voting power and abilities to communicate with each other and with their own state's federal politicians in Washington to demand that The American public be given the opportunity to review the Congressional ethics policy and make suggestions as to what the rules and ethics should be from the elected politicians in Washington D.C. Letting Congress write its own ethics policy and administer that policy with setting elected officials is like putting the Fox in the hen house to guard the Chickens: It will not work and the American Voters will be the losers in this game. Even if an honest person makes it into a Washington political group, the tempentations from Lobbyist and other Washington politicians to play the Washington political game would be difficult for any human being to resist.

A couple of reasons the Washington politicians have developed into the current circumstances is because in the past, the American public did not have any easy form of communicating with their own states Washington politicians other than letters and a few town meetings every now and then. I am sure the Average American did not have any opportunity to review or comment on the ethics policy for Congress, being written and administered by the Washington politicians. This problem or lack of communication ability made it so easy for politicians to play the games that are played in Washington D.C. Large corporations or companies that may have special interest in certain bills that are either before Congress are may be coming before Congress in the future have been known to give either the politician or the politicians' family a special deal on the companies stock. That sort of game playing is illegal in the real world but ok in the congressional ethics policies.

This is why in addition to giving the American Voter an opportunity to review the Congressional ethics policy, the American Voter needs to use the power of their vote to demand their states' Representatives and Senator in Congress pass laws creating a Congressional ethics Committee that is not made up of politicians that are currently holding office.

There are several ways this Congressional Ethics committee could be developed and determining the best way should have a great deal of input from the American Voter.

One way to accomplish this would be for Congress to pass a bill giving the governor of each state the authority to appoint two individuals from each state to serve on a new Congressional Ethics Task Force. The Governor's appointees would have to be approved by their own states' Senate and House of Representatives. I would suggest that these Governor appointees must qualify for the position by having a Bachelor of Science degree from a 4 year accredited college in the United States, preferably in accounting and law, as well as having served in one of the United States Armed Services with an honorable discharge. I would suggest that Veterans which have been wounded in battle should be given first consideration also. The men and women that have served in the military will be good at monitoring the actions of Congress. This job will be as important as fighting on the front lines for democracy either at home or overseas.

This New 100 person Congressional Ethics Task Force would be a full time job for its members who should have the authority to change or correct the Congressional Ethics Policy with finial approval of that policy requireing a majority vote of the 50 American Governors. This Congressional ethics committee would elect its own president and 12 person board to be responsible for the organization of the committee. The Committee responsibility would be to make sure that the elected officials in Washington follow these policies and most importantly make sure that the American public remains informed of what is taking place in our nations capital. This committee should have the authority to act as a police force, to make sure the Washington politician's actions are honest and for the benefit of the American voter rather than the politicians own financial gain. The governor of each state along with each states' Comprotroller's office should have the responsibility to police the Congressional Ethics Task Force actions too make sure that the members of this state controlled task force are acting in a professional manner with ethics that is determined by the state governors as well as approved by the individual states senate and house. Instead of Congress watching what Congress does, the Congressional Ethics Task Force should be watching the Washington Politicians, with the State Governors watching the Congressional Ethics Task Force, and all three parties being responsible to keep the American Voters informed with the motto that "The Public Has a Right to Know".

A large and long book could be written on the Congressional Ethics Task Force as well as what is the best way to handle the current problems of corruption and lack of concern for what is best for the majority of Americans by our leaders in Washington D.C. Remember the current method of placing the fox in the hen house to guard the chickens is going to continue to result in the American Voters being taken advantage of as many times in the future as it has occurred in the past. The American Voter must show their concern with letters emails, and any form of communication to their States Federal Senator and Representative in Congress to change the way the Congressional ethics policy is handled. I am sure the members of Congress will be against the idea of a Congressional Ethics task Force, saying that it will cost the American tax payer even more money increasing the budget. I think the cost of the task force will be a drop in the bucket of the federal budget when compared to what is saves the Tax Payers by keeping a closer watch on America's Congress make sure the American Tax Payer dollars are spent properly by keeping the tax payers in each individual state informed on what is actually going on in Congress. After all, during the past history of America, particularity in the old west, as the country grew, when a town became corrupt and a danger to its citizens, the citizens of that community would elect a new sheriff, sometimes bring the sheriff in from out of town, to clean up their community. That is basically what the American Tax Payer is going to have to do with the political leaders in Washington D.C. We need to bring in a task force, responsible to the elected leaders of each state, a task force that remains in communication with all tax payers from their state, to be honest Americans that clean up the problems with the leaders of the American Government. The current systems in place for this purpose are not getting the job done!

American Voters should also be asking the Senators and Representatives from their individual state for information pertaining to lobbyist money and campaign contributions received by their Congressional leaders. This will be good information to have when checking on how the leaders vote on various issues during their term in office. Another interesting fact to check on your states federal politicians is to find out how much money they are being paid as a consultant or board member for various companies and organizations.

At any rate, if the American Voter does not begin to participate in at least a 99% voting rate on election day, as well as begin to open the lines of communication between the American Voter and their members in Congress, making Congress realize their actions are being monitored by the voters that elected them to office, than the majority of the Average Americans, the middle class and poverty level voters are sure to be the people that suffer the most. If we don't vote and do not keep tract of our Senators and Representatives actions in Congress, then we have no one to blame other than ourselves. We are the generation that has the communication abilities at our disposal that no other American generation has ever had before! It is our responsibility as Americans to stand up use the new forms of communication to turn this nation's economic conditions in the right direction before it is too late for America to survive!

CHAPTER 16

In Summary

America has many many different problems at this time. There is not any one person or political party that can even begin to get our nations business in order. The politicians have known that by creating various issues to excite the public during elections while avoiding the discussions of the real issues where the politician is taking advantage of the American Citizens is a good election strategy. Our national leaders know that by policing their own actions, they can all get away with a lot more for themselves. Many Americans have come to feel like Washington DC Politicians are in such a mess that there is nothing the individual American can do so they just give up trying because the American Voter has so many problems of their own to contend with such as financial problems, health problems, work problems, family problems, and etc. With all the various individual problems that Americans have that has made it even easier in the past for our politicians to keep the public opinions down and let the politician get away with whatever they seem to want to do for the politicians' own benefit.

I am sure that if the Washington politicians ever heard of this "Three Steps" plan to allow Americans to get control of our Washington Politicians they would come up with thousands of reasons these "Three Steps" will not work. The politician will try to throw out smoke screens and create confusion to keep Americans from coming together, voting and keeping up with what the politician from their own state is doing. This has been pretty easy for the politician to accomplish in the past because of the many differences of opinion in American and the inability for All Americans to communicate with each other in a almost instance type response system. Face book, twitter, and email have fixed that problem if Americans will only use these forms of communication and take an interest in what is going on a daily basis in Washington. Even though Americans do have many different opinions and agendas, it would be a lot better if our political leaders are making decisions based on the American voters ideas and opinions rather than the current method of making a political decision in Washington based on how much money the lobbyist, corporation, or foreign government is going to give the Politian.

Sometimes it is difficult *"to see the forest before the trees"* but if every American will give some time and effort to:

Step: 1

Contacting their Federal representatives requesting Congress to pass a bill making The Federal Election Day a National Holiday in America. Our Federal Politicians should know that if the Federal Election Day is not a National Holiday the next time their term is up for re-election, we will be voting for their opponent. We should continue that voting policy until the Federal Election Day is made a National Holiday.

Step: 2

The American Voters should stay in touch with the Senator and House of Representatives for the voters' individual state. The voters should voice their opinions to their congressional representatives.

Step: 3

If the 236,000,000 eligible voters contacted their Congressional representatives and Senators in Washington D.C. continuing to request and demand some reasonable plan to create a non political Congressional Control organization to oversee the ethics of our Federal Politicians rather than the politicians overseeing their own actions, the power of those 236,000,000 million votes could change Washington D.C. Politics forever.

The future of America is up to the 236,000,000 eligible American Voters. Each eligible American voter should honor the lives of our ancestors and children that have fought in various wars over the history of this nation by casing our vote in every election. Thousands of our ancestors have given their lives in battle for the purpose of maintaining the American Citizens' Freedom and right to elect the leaders of this nation, All eligible American Voters must accept going to the election polls to vote on Election Day as his or her responsibility as an American Citizen. We are also going to have to let our Washington D.C. politicians know that we are watching them and holding them accountable for their actions in Washington D.C. by using the new forms of communication we now have available.

The American Voters need to let the politician know what bills or laws the American Voters want to see discussed in Washington DC. The American Voter needs to keep up with their own states' Washington D.C. Politician's web site in order to remain informed as to what bills and laws their Congressional Representatives and Senators are working on. On a regular and consistent basis, the American Voter should be sending emails, face book or twitter comments to keep their Congressional Representative and Senators informed of the voters' opinions and thoughts concerning the current issues before Congress. The American Voter must let their politician know that Congress is working for the 236,000,000 voters in America, not the lobbyist, campaign contributors, and money that comes to Washington D.C. politicians from various sources. Former United States President **Woodrow Wilson** made this statement when he was in office,

"The ear of the leader must ring with the voices of the people".

So stand up American Voters, take interest in America's business and take control over the actions of America's elected officials! After all, it is the American Voters' tax dollars the politicians are spending!

If America is going to survive in the future, the only group that can save this nation is the American Voter! If the American Voters don't step up by exercising their right to vote, and exercise the American Voter's right to contact the Congress person representing the state they live in for the purpose of keeping those elected official informed of the American Voter's opinions, than no one else will be able to save America from the greed and corruption that goes on in Washington D.C.!

AFTERWORD

Many people believe that history repeats itself. One would think if we understood history, we'd figure out ways to prevent the bad parts from reoccurring and only allow the good to repeat.

Over 200 years ago our founding fathers and ancestors left Europe in search of a better life, for both theirselves and future generations. They left a world of tyranny and oppression of freedoms ranging from religion, speech, thought, choice of work, expression, day to day life choices, even the oppression of the mere pursuit of happiness, and the oppression to hope and dream of a better tomorrow. They embarked on a voyage to a new world, one undeveloped, vastly undiscovered, and one they knew little about. They embarked on the voyage in hopes of living a life free of the oppressions, with the ability and power to chose their own ways, create their own live and paths, worship, think, and believe however they saw fit, and also to create the possibility for future generations to live a life far greater than they could imagine. Above all, our founding fathers and ancestors wanted to write their own story.

In exchange for the chance to have freedoms and to be able to write their own story, our Founders and Ancestors were willing to risk it all and even make the ultimate sacrifice, death. Not only was the act of traveling across the world and living in unforeseen conditions risky and sometimes fatal, but even once the colonies had been established our founders still ran the risk of losing it all. If the colonies and George Washington would have lost the Revolution, our founding fathers and colonists would have been executed. Imagine if policy makers today ran the same risk our founders did.

Many brave souls did make the ultimate sacrifice during the Revolution, so that America could not just win a war, but so that her and her people could simply have a chance. During our founding years, nobody knew for certain America would succeed, they just knew it was better than the alternatives and that above all else they had to give it a chance. From the Revolution to the Civil War, to the World Wars to Korea, to the jungles of Vietnam, to today in Iraq and Afghanistan and the war on terror, brave souls are still making the ultimate sacrifice so that America and her people will not become oppressed, so that we can still live in freedom, and so that America can still have a chance. As a society, we should honor these 200 plus years of sacrifice by making the most of the chance that has been bestowed upon us.

While it hasn't been perfect, every generation of America since our fore fathers founding have left the country in better shape than they found it, not only did they pass the chance of America on to the next generation, they gave them a better one. However, many recent polls show that most parents today don't think that their children will have the same quality of life that they have experienced as Americans. Unprecedented national debt, high unemployment(particularly among young people, and in rural America) increase costs of living, 11 straight years of negative job growth with simultaneous global expansion due to U.S. policies, irresponsible foreign and domestic policies that put the entire world only one act, one second away from total destruction, and a government bureaucracy that's made up of the ultra wealthy, a government that is so broken it can't agree upon what day of the week it is, a government whose policies and political posturing has not only helped create all these problems, but also doesn't seem to mind passing them on to the next generation to deal with, doesn't give one much hope that tomorrow will be better than today. When history writes about those of us that live today, both older and younger, do we want to be the ones that not only failed America, but failed each other and the ones to come after us?

Common knowledge lets us know that when you use something in a way that it wasn't intended to be used for, it's going have problems or break. This is what has happened with our political system. Our founders didn't design the system to be a two party ideology based system, or one made up of elitist, or one that excludes the majority of the citizens. These are part of the oppressions they left behind in Europe and what inspired them to found America. They warned us not to let America take this route and why it's a bad idea. George Washington made it clear in his farewell speech why America should not result to party based ideological politics—*"They serve to Organize faction, to give it an artificial and extraordinary force—to put in the place of the delegated will of the Nation, the will of a party; often a small but artful and enterprising minority of the Community; and, according to the alternate triumphs of different parties, to make the public Administration the Mirror of the ill concerted and incongruous projects of faction, rather than the Organ of consistent and wholesome plans digested by common councils and modified by mutual interests. However combinations or Associations of the above description may now & then answer popular ends, they are likely, in the course of time and things, to become potent engines, by which cunning, ambitious and unprincipled men will be enabled to subvert the Power of the People, & to usurp for themselves the reins of Government; destroying afterwards the very engines which have lifted them to unjust dominion . . . .*

It serves always to distract the Public Councils and enfeeble the Public Administration. It agitates the Community with ill founded Jealousies and false alarms, kindles the animosity of one part against another, foments occasionally riot & insurrection. It opens the door to foreign influence & corruption, which find a facilitated access to the government itself through the channels of party passions. Thus the policy and the will of one country, are subjected to the policy and will of another. – George Washington Farewell Address"

For generations Americans have prided their selves on freedom and innovation. We created the automobile, modern flight, put men on the moon, cured diseases, created instant communication with anyone, anytime, anywhere in the world, more than 100 flavors of ice cream and 74 colors of crayons, and 20 different combo meals at a fast food restaurant, yet we force all of our politics into a box with only 2 sides. Our problems are too big for our current left or right approach to governance and what we risk losing by not solving these problems is even bigger. Our founding fathers left us with the greatest weapon in the world. Not a military, not the right to bear arms, not the freedom of religion or speech, but the ability and obligation as citizens to rise up and change the direction of our government, the power of the pen and the power of the vote, so that even in the darkest of times we still have the power to write our own story. *"We hold these truths to be self-evident, that all men are created equal, that they are endowed by their Creator with certain unalienable Rights, that among these are Life, Liberty and the pursuit of Happiness.—That to secure these rights, Governments are instituted among Men, deriving their just powers from the consent of the governed,—That whenever any Form of Government becomes destructive of these ends, it is the Right of the People to alter or to abolish it, and to institute new Government, laying its foundation on such principles and organizing its powers in such form, as to them shall seem most likely to effect their Safety and Happiness."*

President Bill Clinton once said that *"if he learned anything at all, it was that everyone has a story . . . . And that he always felt the main point of his work was to give people a chance to have better stories"*. It's time for Americans to have better stories. Instead of stories of lost jobs, homes, and families, loss of a voice in government, loss of hope for a better future for the next generation, it's time for the stories of triumph, innovations, participation in democracy, sustainability, security, prosperity, and the chance to hope that tomorrows stories will be better than today's. However, these happy ending stories will never be told if average everyday Americans don't take back our pens, voices, and votes, and write our own stories rather than hoping for out of touch career elitist politicians in Washington that couldn't even agree upon what font to use, to tell the story for us.

BIOGRAPHY

Freddy Bishop and his wife Cheryl have two grown children and one son-in-law. Freddy is retired after spending 4 years in the retail business and 31 years in the natural gas industry. Freddy's college degree is in business administration.